Love Notes

FROM ME TO YOU

FROM

_____

TO

_____

What I'm looking forward to in life with you is ...

_____

_____

_____

_____

_____

_____

I respect your ...

_____

_____

_____

_____

_____

_____

I love it when we play …

_____

_____

_____

_____

_____

_____

_____

If I was to give you any award, it would be for …

_____

_____

_____

_____

_____

_____

_____

What I love about your sense of humor is ...

_____

_____

_____

_____

_____

_____

_____

It still amazes me, the story of how you ...

_____

_____

_____

_____

_____

_____

_____

TO

ME,

YOU

ARE ...

One of my favorite times with you was ...

_____

_____

_____

_____

_____

_____

You're sexy when you ...

_____

_____

_____

_____

_____

_____

I'm so grateful you ...

_____

_____

_____

_____

_____

_____

_____

**If I could choose one trait of yours to adopt
as my own it would be ...**

_____

_____

_____

_____

_____

_____

_____

Love recognizes no barriers.
It jumps hurdles, leaps fences,
penetrates walls to arrive at its
destination full of hope.

– Maya Angelou

I love it when you ...

_____

_____

_____

_____

_____

_____

One thing I'd love to do with you again is ...

_____

_____

_____

_____

_____

_____

I'm obsessed with your ...

_____

_____

_____

_____

_____

_____

_____

My favorite thing about you is your ...

_____

_____

_____

_____

_____

_____

_____

You've always stood apart to me because of your ...

_____

_____

_____

_____

_____

_____

_____

Around you, I feel ...

_____

_____

_____

_____

_____

_____

_____

I love how every day, you ...

_____

_____

_____

_____

_____

_____

_____

Five words that come to mind when I think about you are ...

1. _____

2. _____

3. _____

4. _____

5. _____

One of your most attractive
physical features is your ...

_____

_____

_____

_____

_____

_____

_____

What I admire most about you is your ...

_____

_____

_____

_____

_____

_____

_____

Five ways you've brought out the best in me are ...

1. _____

_____

_____

2. _____

_____

_____

3. _____

_____

_____

4. _____

_____

_____

5. _____

_____

_____

Without you ...

_____

_____

_____

_____

_____

_____

_____

What I love most about being with you is ...

_____

_____

_____

_____

_____

_____

_____

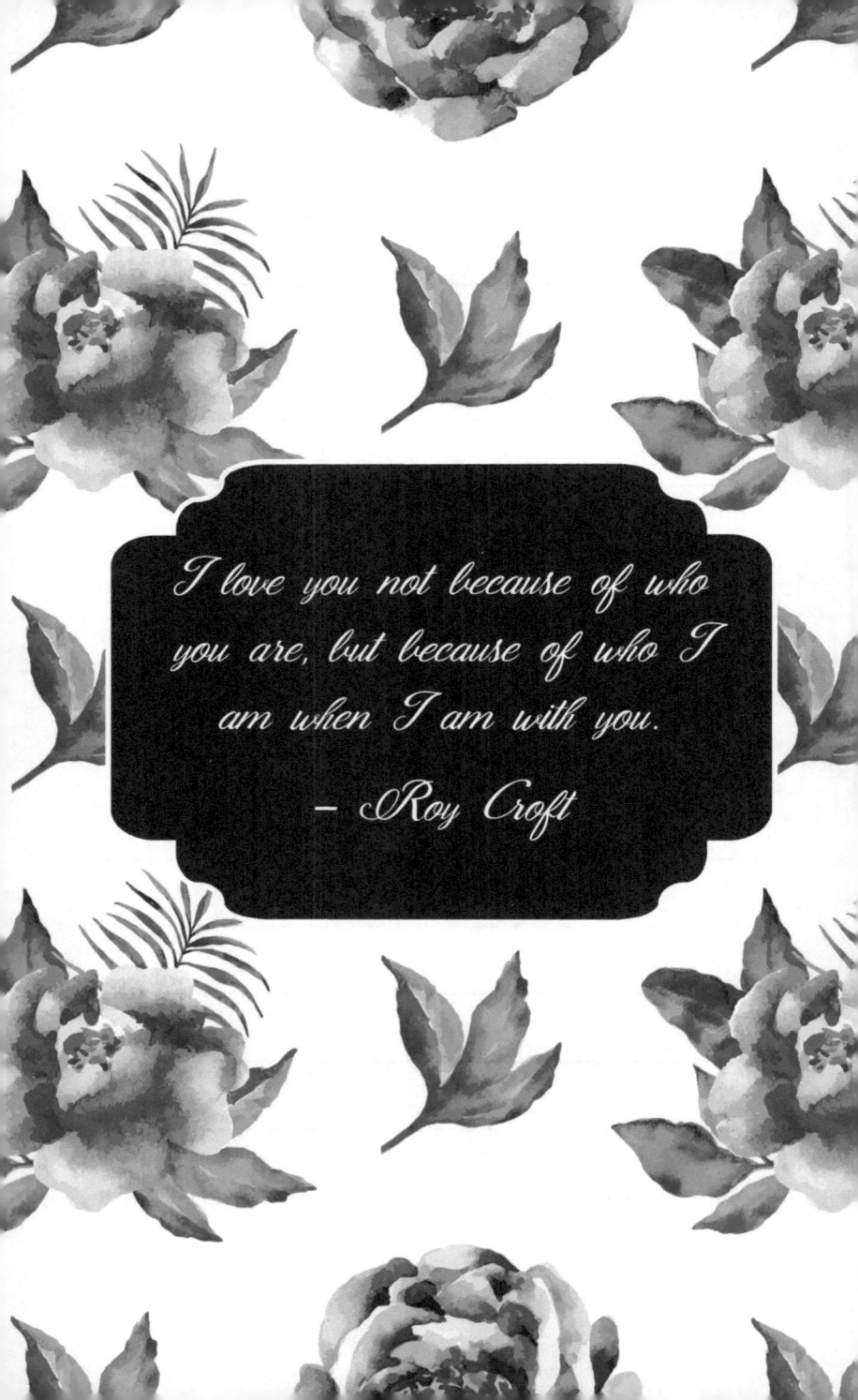

I love you not because of who you are, but because of who I am when I am with you.

— Roy Croft

I love when you call me ...

_____

_____

_____

_____

_____

_____

The best part of arguing with you is ...

_____

_____

_____

_____

_____

_____

Some of your quirks I find endearing are ...

_____

_____

_____

_____

_____

_____

Every day with you is ...

_____

_____

_____

_____

_____

_____

I couldn't live without your ...

_____

_____

_____

_____

_____

_____

The best thing someone else has said about you is ...

_____

_____

_____

_____

_____

_____

I LOVE
THAT
YOU
WERE
THERE
WHEN ...

I still get butterflies when you ...

_____

_____

_____

_____

_____

_____

When I'm with you, I love to share ...

_____

_____

_____

_____

_____

_____

You've taught me so much about ...

_____

_____

_____

_____

_____

_____

This quote makes me think of you ...

_____

_____

_____

_____

_____

_____

One thing I've learned from you is ...

_____

_____

_____

_____

_____

_____

Little things you do that I love include ...

_____

_____

_____

_____

_____

_____

You're so gifted at ...

_____

_____

_____

_____

_____

_____

_____

I believe that if you really wanted, you could ...

_____

_____

_____

_____

_____

_____

I love how you're not afraid to ...

_____

_____

_____

_____

_____

_____

You're so caring ...

_____

_____

_____

_____

_____

_____

No matter the difficulty, you ...

_____

_____

_____

_____

_____

_____

_____

You never stop ...

_____

_____

_____

_____

_____

_____

_____

Love is friendship
that has caught fire.

– Ann Landers

I love going ...

_____

_____

_____

_____

_____

_____

_____

Making love with you is ...

_____

_____

_____

_____

_____

_____

When I think of you, I ...

_____

_____

_____

_____

_____

_____

I hope you know just how much ...

_____

_____

_____

_____

_____

_____

I love that you help ...

_____

_____

_____

_____

_____

_____

I love when you say ...

_____

_____

_____

_____

_____

_____

You being vulnerable with me means ...

_____

_____

_____

_____

_____

_____

You really show me who you are when ...

_____

_____

_____

_____

_____

_____

What surprised me the most when we were first getting to know each other was ...

_____

_____

_____

_____

_____

_____

_____

What surprises me most about you now is ...

_____

_____

_____

_____

_____

_____

You exposed me to ...

_____

_____

_____

_____

_____

_____

I know your future is bright because ...

_____

_____

_____

_____

_____

_____

It's so romantic when you ...

_____

_____

_____

_____

_____

_____

_____

Your _____ is the best.

I
WANT
YOU
TO
KNOW ...

MY FAVORITE PICTURE OF US:

Made in United States
Troutdale, OR
01/05/2024

16718103R00030